Quadrille

QUADRILLE

Christianity and the Early
New England Indians

Diane Glancy

RESOURCE *Publications* • Eugene, Oregon

QUADRILLE
Christianity and the Early New England Indians

Copyright © 2024 Diane Glancy. All rights reserved. Except for brief quotations in critical publications or reviews, no part of this book may be reproduced in any manner without prior written permission from the publisher. Write: Permissions, Wipf and Stock Publishers, 199 W. 8th Ave., Suite 3, Eugene, OR 97401.

Resource Publications
An Imprint of Wipf and Stock Publishers
199 W. 8th Ave., Suite 3
Eugene, OR 97401

www.wipfandstock.com

PAPERBACK ISBN: 979-8-3852-1103-6
HARDCOVER ISBN: 979-8-3852-1104-3
EBOOK ISBN: 979-8-3852-1105-0

VERSION NUMBER 04/24/24

Quadrille—

as in quad [four parts]

as in drill [military]— as in John Eliot's efforts
to bring Indian languages
into subjugation with RULES of the English language—

as opposed to the freedom of motion in
the historical dance called

Quadrille [though it also has its rules].

Contents

THE FLYING HEAD or the Nightmare of Christianity | 1
    The beginning of them with Christians—
    The Flying Head Put to Flight by a Woman Parching Acorns | 2
    What the Matter with Them? | 4
    Praying Indians | 5
    When the Gravy is Consumed | 7

NEW ENGLAND INDIANS | 9
    Four Native men translate the 1663 Algonquian Bible
        with John Eliot—
    John Eliot | 14
    Cockenoe, Montauk | 17
    Wowaus or James Printer, Nipmuc | 21
    John Sassamon, Massachusett | 26
    Job Nesuton, Massachusett | 28

I, TATAMY | 31
    Moses Tenda Tauta-my [c.1690-1760], Lenape interpreter for
    David Brainerd, missionary to the New England Indians

THE CONVERSION OF HE GOES FIRST,
DAVID PENDLETON OAKERHATER | 61
    One of the 72 Plains Indian warriors imprisoned at Fort
    Marion in St. Augustine, Florida, 1875-1878

Acknowledgments, Notes and Bibliography | 75

THE FLYING HEAD

Or the Nightmare of Christianity

From David Cusick's sketches of ancient history of the Six Nations, 1842, *Illustration* from *Myths of the Iroquois*, Erminne A. Smith (1863-1866), Anthropologist, Bureau of American Ethnology, Smithsonian Institution

The Flying Head Put to Flight by a Woman Parching Acorns

If I work. And work. The Flying Head would. Take his puffy head. If I roast acorns. If I not look. He might shut his teethy mouth. If I ignore. If I parch my acorns in the fire. If I write. My own version. He won't. On his four-clawed feet. My little fire hot. He cannot interrupt. He can't hone in. He have no arms. If I parch. If I put hand to mouth. He take his awful head on feet. He have short legs. Neck gone. He growl. AAAAHHHHHH-HHRRRRRRRRRRRRR. If I keep stick in fire. Feet on ground. If I keep back to him. He not there.

What the Matter with Them?

Somehow they come. We did not ask. Their ships arrove and did not have a place to stay. They camp with us. They hungry. We say plant crops. Most dead by spring. But more ships flung. Move over. The animals they brung— cow, sheep, hog. Our people dead of smallpox. We have message from God, they say. Hold Jesus on stick. There are cornfields in heaven. See the clouds in rows of corn. Why they keep coming? It was trouble with them. They fought for land. It was unto us to do the same. But ground was lost. We knowd not what to do. Some went to the God they brought. Seeing something beyond the ships that flopped on shore. They wade. To see words written on a page. They said were words that made them live forever.

Praying Indians[1]

God had a book. There were three Gods in the book. The book opened to One God making people. They were bad. One God tied Two God to a tree. It was the One God's way to cook. It was all we understood. Wolves would waltz at Two God's marriage supper. Foxes barked the wedding song. Three God came when Two God was gone on his trip. He had his spelling lessons already done. We rowed a canoe. He said the book was a world we would know when we got there.

Deer Island, Boston Harbor, The Province of Massachusetts, 1675, to keep Christian Indians from King Philip's War, also called Metacomet, whom New England Colonists pushed to the wall until he was hostile and vengeful— They sent us to an island named deer-swam-there-when-wolves-chased-them. 500-1000 Nipmuc from the Praying Towns. Converted by John Eliot. By December the cold wind opened the top of the ocean. The teeth

---

1. Praying Towns were established by the Massachusetts Bay Colony between 1651 and 1674— sometimes in villages already established. The Reverend John Eliot and other Puritan leaders believed that these towns would allow them to isolate and manage potential converts in order to completely change Native ways. Natives who went to live in the towns gained material assistance, education, and deeper connections to the Colonists and their God. Natick was the first praying town, followed by six others in a north-south arc west of Boston— Gay Head and Christiantown on Martha's Vineyard. Nantucket. Mashpee, Grafton, Plymouth and Herring Pond. Residents were required to follow a legal code designed to force them into English social and political patterns. Christian Indians led each town, although Eliot and Bay Colony officials supervised their actions— Wikipedia

chewed our hands. We built a fire but the wind blew it away. This is what we have against you. Our faces blue with cold. Inlets of the ocean swallowing half of us.

When the Gravy Is Consumed

From the Second Report of the Bureau of Ethnology to the Secretary of the Smithsonian Institution 1880-81 by J.W. Powell, Director [Washington, Government Printing Office, 1883]— I write you this report. Not all well in the field. There is bezzelment. I don't know what to call it. How to spell. The whole place amuck with infestors. Wing it, Sir, I do. Interrupt, Sire, into these eternal postings. Intrude. With my own thoughts. My own fears. Of worlds not seen. We give them our unseen— Father Son and Holy Ghost. They have their unseen. Monsters I tell you. If I can enlist my thoughts and feelings. We are in danger here. In the vast unknown. Until we are nothing, Sir, nothing. When this in the hereafter is sort out, Sir, the first dance of the purified will be Theirs.

Translation— for Joseph Brant, *Thayendanegea* [he places two bets], Mohawk, 1743-1807, Interpreter for the Missionary John Stuart— and Translator of the Book of Mark— To translate a story into another language is to make a likeness of a likeness. *A voice crying in the wilderness.* Those words Brant knew. The Mohawk languished over the Colonists. Maybe the English would take them back. Maybe they would run over a cliff into the sea. To translate is to saw through a thick tree. It is to hear a *misery-whip*, one pulling, one pushing, separating tree from stump. And what is heard as they tear apart is translation—

NEW ENGLAND INDIANS

The four translators of the 1663 Algonquian Bible—

Cockenoe, Montauk
Wowaus or James Printer, Nipmuc
John Sassamon, Massachusett
Job Nesuton, Massachusett

Kah namehteoog qussuk tuttuppequanausu wutch wenohkit
—Luke XXIV 2

And they found the stone rolled away from the sepulcher
—Luke 24:2

There are words that are feral.
There are words that are tame.
I would rather the tame than the feral.
Do not take the feral with the tame.
This should be understood before the trip begins.
There is an assortment in packing.
What animal to put into what pen.
They come to the New World only to be eaten by
    the wild animals that fight among themselves
    and the outcome hardly ever approachable.

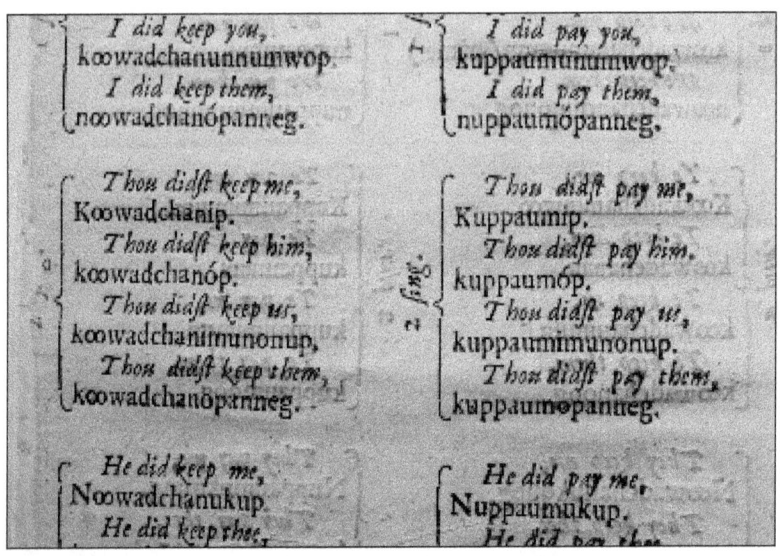

From John Eliot's "The Indian Grammar Begun, or an Essay to bring the Indian Language into RULES . . . for the furtherance of the Gospel among them"

The Reverend John Eliot [1609-1690] came to the Massachusetts Bay Colony from London in 1631. He pastored the Roxbury Church near Boston for 60 years.

One of his missions in the New World was to convert the indigenous to Christianity.

The barrier to preaching to Indians was language.

Eliot decided that if the Indians could hear the Gospel in their own language, they would understand God's message. He began studying the Algonquian language of the Massachusett Indian, a language that had no written form. For fourteen years he translated the 66 books of the English Bible into Algonquian with the help of four Native men—

1. Cockenoe, Montauk
2. Wowaus or James Printer, Nipmuc
3. John Sassamon, Massachusett
4. Job Nesuton, Massachusett

> *For the Conftruction of words* together, *I will give three fhort Rules.*
>
> 1. VVHen *two Nouns come together*, one of them is turned into a kinde of an Adverb, or Adnoun, and that is an *Elegancy* in the Language: of which fee frequent Examples. See 1 *Pet.*2.2. Pahkefogkodtungane wuttinnowaonk; *The pure milkie word*, for *Milk of the word.* The like may be obferved a thoufand times.
>
> 2. When *two Verbs come together*, the latter is the *Infinitive Mode*: as in the fame 1 *Pet.*2.5. Kooweekikoniteeamwoo fephaufinat. *Ye are built,* &c. *to facrifice,* &c. And a thoufand times more this Rule occurs.

John Eliot—

How could the sounds of the Algonquian language be written in words? How could Native language be established from nothing but the tame words of the English? There were nouns and pronouns and verbs and adjectives and adverbs and prepositions and conjunctions and interjections. There were all degrees of them. How to put the feral sound of utterance from the Indians into the proper use? How to put tame language over the feral when the feral was fiercer? Often the feral fought back, though it was for their benefit they were being tamed.

I had a twerk of pain in my head. Along the left side of my face.

I had to decipher their language. I had to tame it with the English RULES of grammar. I had to shape and reshape and insert words that did not want to go into the Algonquian language. It was the RULES of grammar that were in more trouble than the Indian language that resisted the English.

In a nightmare one night, the Algonquian language was stalking my work. It was outside. The door was closed and secured. The baby had stopped crying. My wife returned to bed. But the nightmare could turn sideways and fit through the smallest crack between the door and its frame.

I had to realize how tedious the work also for them. I had to look at the language and the four Indians who understood it and were unwilling sometimes to do the arduous task of sitting at the desk all day pondering over the written word while inside they were vying between Indian and Colonist allegiance.

I went over verses again and again.

The men were hungry. They were tired. They were restless. They rallied.

We worked through another verse. With discussion. How to fit the thought into Algonquian that did not want the thought.

I had to rethink how language worked. I had to think how Christianity worked.

thy name	come	thy kingdom
koowesuonk	peyaumooutch	kukketetassootamoonk

[from Matthew 6:9-10]

There were changes in sound hardly noticeable to me that were the differences between light and dark— death and life.

It was a tide pool in which we were caught.

How to put the feral animals of Native speech into transitive and intransitive and all the units of grammar.

I wanted the waves in my nightmare to wash me into oblivion.

Ketoohomaonk. XXXIII.
yeuweto wunnaewontammoo-
oukahnoowoash missinninuog.
 11 Ukkenoosoowaonk Je-
hovah michemkompatteau,
wuttahhe unnantamooonkash
en wame pometuonkanash.
 12 Wunnantamun wutah-
timoin wa-Manittoomut Je-
hovah: kah missinninnuh neh
pepenaunhpoh wutche nehen-
wonche ootohtoonganinauh.
 13 Jehovah womompu
wurch kesukqut, nauwau wa-
me wunnaumonaoh woske-
tompaog.

Psalm. XXXIII.
devices of the people of none
effect.
 11 The counsel of the
Lord standeth for ever, the
thoughts of his heart to all
generations.
 12 Blessed is the nation
whose God is the Lord: and
the people whom he hath
chosen for his own inhe-
ritance.
 13 The Lord looketh
from heaven: he beholdeth
all the sons of men.

ONE
Cockenoe [Montauk]—

We sit at a table. The open Bible is before us.
The Lord looketh from heaven— Psalm 33:13.
There is no word in Algonquian for Lord.
There is no word for heaven. There is a word for look.
Who shall we say looks? Where shall we say he looks from?
These words were brought from across the water.
These words we do not know.
But they had come. We had to look at them.
They were running over us.
But there was something running to us also.
A message of salvation.
The European God had trampled over the waves.
He overcame fish.
His people crossed an ocean that could swallow them.
That could push its water into their mouths and stifle
    the breath in them.
It seemed there was a heavy fog in the room as if it came
    from the sea.
The dark green walls were a forest that pushed in on us.
I held to the table to let its hardness hold me so I would not
    float away in the fog and be lost forever.
But that was the message.

The Lord, while he was taking our land, was providing a way
  we would not be lost forever—though we had not known
  we were lost forever.
But if we believed in Him, He saved our soul.
The Lord was telling us we had a soul He would save.
He was telling us He was looking down on us.
To help us.
The room was smaller than when we first sat down.
We could sit at the table for a while and then had to get up.
From time to time we had to leave the room that was
  pulling us drowned into their sea.

Cockenoe [continued]

It was faith— John Eliot said.
I could believe in something I couldn't see.
But Indians believed that way.
There was a whole world invisible to sight— Spirits moved.
Trees talked.
It was a fearful world.
We had enough of it.
We knew the invisible world more than they did.
We knew it and were afraid of it.
But there was an upside to Eliot's invisible world.
The Evil one was there, but the emphasis was on God.
The three of Him— Father.Son.HolyGhost.
It was hard to understand.
It pulled up the roots of our way of thinking that always
    had been.
Eliot said it was faith that brought the Colonists across the ocean.
It took a long time.
Two full moons passed over the ship, Eliot said.
I wanted his faith.
It was the words of the Bible Eliot read.
I felt them inside.
Others scoffed, but I believed.

When we were near to giving up the work of translation—
   Eliot rallied us.
He heard our utterances and knew there was disagreement.
We muffled our speech to hide it from him.
We were battered in the storm as we debated our allegiances
   to Native and Christian worlds.

How could they use three letters to write the name of their
   G.o.d? How could they write his name in such a small way?
Three letters because he was three?—
We would write him as Him.who.is.all.of.all.
Who.is.all.of.whom.there.is.all.
Of.whom.is.known.little.
Him.who.is.here.but.not.to.be.known.

The Christian message was harder.
We had sinned [what was sin?] which kept us from heaven [for which it is established there is no word in Algonquian] but God killed his son on the cross [they had a God that tortured] and in the shedding of blood, was the propitiation for sin [how would we say that in Algonquian?] and whoso believed the story is rescued from being lost forever and placed in the heaven above.

What to know about translating—

1. Trees have to be cleared.
2. A road has to be carved.
3. The cart and horse have to be built.
4. And the day in which they exist.

TWO

Wowaus or James Printer [Nipmuc] (d. 1717)—

Then Seawaters gathereth in a heap— Psalm 33:7

> BOSTON, N. E.
> Printed by *B. Green*, and *J. Printer*, for the Honourable COMPANY for the Propagation of the Gofpel in *New-England*, &c.
> 1 7 0 9.

James Printer's name appears in the translation of Genesis, Psalms, Matthew, where Eliot began his work. None of the Native men are given credit in the Indian [or Algonquian] Bible for their work of translation.

What was it like for them to sit there so long? And what was it like for James Printer to place the letters of the Algonquian language into the rows on the printing press in Cambridge? In the English Bible, there are 783,137 words. There are 3,116,480 characters. The Algonquian Bible was not short-cutted, but printed in its entirety.

James Printer—

I lined up stones on the shore of the creek as a boy.
I liked to arrange shapes.

When I saw the metal letters of the alphabet in the sections
    of the printer's drawer—
    they were pebbles on the shore.
The memory returned of putting one stone beside another
    to make a long row.

I liked the rows on the press into which I put the letters.
It was the creek I had known as a boy.
I remembered the little wave-lines on the shore.
Sometimes the rows hardened when the mud dried.
I touched them with my finger.
Already I was putting the letters in their places.

The great handle on the press was a tree branch I swung on—
It all came back.
Printing was nothing more than boyhood returned to me.
Once they had been separate—the branch and the stones
   from the creek—
   now they were linked in printing.
I liked the patient work of placing letters in rows on the press—

the letters in a word placed backwards to print the pages
    of the Bible.
It was a ship that carried the printing press.
A ship that brought the New World.

I was alone by the creek those mornings and afternoons I worked.
The stones were putting themselves in my hands.

James Printer [continued]

The printing press was taller than a man.
It was bolted to the floor and ceiling so it wouldn't walk
   when I pulled the handle.

I took the metal letters from their compartments.
I placed them on the composition plate I would serve to the press.

I mixed linseed oil with soot wiped from kerosene lamps for ink.

I felt the press was an animal.
Its hooves standing still as paper was placed over
   the composition plate
   and rolled under the press that printed the letters
   our people could read.

As we were held in place as the Colonists marked our land.

I was with the Colonists.
I was with the Nipmuc.
How could I be both?

I wondered what kind of animal— the printing press.
Formed into something it was not.
Putting its black teeth-marks on paper.

Who were these men who thought how to do such things?
And why?—
So spoken words would be seen on paper.
So a voice could be carried in a book.

THREE

John Sassamon [Massachusett]— Betrayal

They landed from the sea.
Why had they fled?—
John Eliot said they wanted a place
    where they could follow their beliefs.
They felt our land was a place from their God.
They only had to land their boats, walk on shore,
    and claim it for their own purposes.
They were surprised to see us.
They were regretful.
There was thought at first of us living side by side.
But they pushed us over.
With promise of compromise.
Of sharing.
It was not theirs to share.
A Sachem, Metacomet, was angered.
He had taken the name, King Philip,
    with respect to his father's kinship with the Colonists.
Now it seemed traitorous.
His anger never gave up.
I went to school.
I taught school.
I showed him this way of life that had come to be tolerable.
But he was a man of war.
I saw him unable to relent.
Metacomet had to withstand the Europeans.

As one deer withstood another deer who came for its territory.
Its herd.
There were choices.
I still held to that thought.
Mine was to acquiesce.
To observe their ways.
To try them.
More ships arrived.
More villages built.
The houses walled.
The fields fenced in open air.
Their cows and pigs strayed.
I saw their way with books.
With words.
With ideas.
It was more than take up bow and arrow and kill.
Metacomet planned an attack[2].
The European military knew.
Maybe I said something to them.
Maybe others.
I heard footsteps of the Wampanoag in the snow.
I heard the crunch of moccasins.
They carried me to the pond.
I heard them break the ice.
I felt the frigid water.
I fought when they held me down— they twisted
 and broke my neck.
I spasmed as they pushed me under the ice.
I saw white deer gather.
They said I could follow them.

---

2. Eventually the English drew and quartered Philip's body and publicly displayed his head on a stake in Plymouth. King Philip's War [1675-1678], which was extremely costly to the Colonists of southern New England, ended Native American dominance in the region and inaugurated a period of unimpeded colonial expansion— Wikipedia.

FOUR

Job Nesuton [Massachusett]—

I fished at the Quinsigamond.

I heard the spirits in a storm.
Others answered from across the hill.
It was the duties they had.
To terrify us.
To turn over every corner until nothing was left and we were flat
    as the surface of the lake.
Though waves were bucking in the storm.
Nothing could stop the spirits.
Except the word—Eliot said.
The word was a bastion.
I held to that thought as the storm passed.

I returned to the wigwam with my string of fish.
The pickerel from the Quinsigamond.

I could see the other wigwams in the full moon.
I could see the fish on the drying rack.
That night, the moon crossed the sky.
I knew the Evil One and his host were in the corners
    of the woods.
Pulling the moon as if a large fish.

Taking a bite of it until it was smaller and smaller.
Then the moon was gone except the bones of its curved spine.
The spirits would fish again when the moon was full in the sky.

There was magic in the angle of light on the water of
    the Quinsigamond.
It looked like small canoes floated there.
Spirits were paddling and the lake hummed as they paddled
    and the small canoes were almost lost among the waves.
But step into the water at night and you feel the sting of
    their hooks in your feet.
The spirits line the shore with their traps.
They bite the shins.
Trying to catch you before you hop back to shore.

The animals of the woods are quiet when the spirits came
    to the water.
A large fist was seen slapping the waves.
A body without arms or legs like a streak of lightning.
Sometimes there was thunder.
We knew the spirits could torment us.
Even if we lit a fire.
But faith would keep the spirits from the wigwam— Eliot said—
    even when the wigwam seemed to move back and forth
    as moonlight on the water.
Sometimes the spirits were in the moonlight.
They had spells thick as fish without arms or legs.
The spirits wore shadows.
They could look like they weren't there— but step outside
    the wigwam
    and they could flatten you with a falling branch
    and take the air out of you
    until you were a blanket.

I had seen a man with the air sucked out of him.
He was on the ground flat as a fish.

I, TATAMY

Turning from that which will not heal
William Catling
2006-2008
Ceramic, wood and wire
90 x 22 x 24
With the signpost—
"Looking down... lame, and waiting for the waters to tremble."[3]

3. ... an angel went down at a certain season into the pool, and troubled the water; whosoever then first, after the rumbling of the water, stepped in was made well of whatever disease he had— John 5:4

ONE

N'dappin— I am here.

It was Tatamy in his field,
    a walking stick for a leg,
    a twig wired to his chest for an arm.
His body—a fat pod.
Or chrysalis from which a head emerged.
He looked away from his torn shoulder
    [it is the past that will not heal].
He stood by the brown furrows running into the distance,
    the twig of his arm from the thorned pepper tree.

TWO

I, TATAMY

[c 1690-1760]

Your fields are still there— in Tatamy, Pennsylvania,
  off Highway 33 north of Bethlehem
  just south of the Stroudsburg exit.

The plowed furrows. The crops planted.

Moses Tenda Tauta-my, Lenni-Lenape the white settlers called Munsee Delaware, became the interpreter for the missionary David Brainerd. In New Jersey, helping Lenape settle land, Tatamy met Brainerd. He had a reputation of being a go-between, an interpreter, a smoother of the bumpy road between Colonist and Indian.

Guttummaukalummeh— have mercy on me—

How could I tell the Lenape what Brainerd preached?
Have mercy in the sense of addressing God, which Brainerd meant.
Have mercy to Colonists who wanted the land.
Have mercy on us who were in the way of their wanting.

It was God that was Brainerd's overriding request.
How could I change the Indians' focus to God by changing
 Brainerd's words into words the Lenape could understand?

It wasn't just the words that were different. But the meaning
 of language.

How long before they knew we were replaced by the Colonists?
How long before the Indians understood the new people
 brought their God to our land?

Brainerd came to tell the Indians the new light by which
 they could understand.
We were to receive the message of encroachment by God
 and his people.

THREE

I, Tatamy, traveled with Brainerd on horseback in cold and rain. We slept on the ground. Often, Brainerd could not stop coughing. I saw the sickness in him. Yet we traveled from place to place to preach the gospel to the Indians— their encampments of bark wigwams and longhouses in clearings.

Have mercy on us— Tatamy, the interpreter, and David Brainerd, early missionary to the Indians, who could not get through a sermon without coughing. I wanted to say, This is what we're here for— we will undo your world and replace it with two others— the Colonists' world and their God's world.

I thought it was hopeless, but I interpreted Brainerd's words. As I spoke his words, a wave swept over the Indians. They knelt on the ground groaning and weeping. Some fell to their knees HOWLING. There was awakening to some new knowledge that belonged to God. A hollow place they had known was there, but did not know how to address.

To others, Brainerd's message was gristle caught in their throat. I saw them leave. But there were those who felt the soul, or whatever that place in us was— a saddlebag or trunk sent overland from a long distance, and delivered directly by a spring-board wagon.

The Indians felt the awakening and cried in its anguish. Hemmed on every side. Brainerd's words were a language in English I had to change into Lenape. While the ANGER rose at being ROBBED of land— there was gratitude at being added to at the same time. The sheer nakedness of having lost a way of life. Of being destitute. Prey to the Colonists' diseases. Without hope it ever would be different. There was comfort in Brainerd's words for the woundings. The Indians understood that more than the Colonists.

Four

History is a coal burning in the light of day.

History is a ship on the sea arriving.
A sea arriving on a ship.

walamoewagan— truth
walamoe— he [it] truth speaks

There is disembarkment—
a washing over—

There is game—
dried, salted, preserved in a smoke-house.

A ledger of new words— hayfork, harrow, plow, claw hatchet.
A meaning of history unlatched.

FIVE

The depth of the Indians' weeping puzzled Brainerd.
He was used to Puritan restraint.
None of them carried on in this manner.

Why hadn't I been as contrite?
I was confident I was in the flock because I confessed Jesus Christ
    as my Savior.
I believed the Promise of his Blood sheltering me.
I was aware of my distress.
I had been a spokesman for the Colonists to the Indians.
An arbitrator.
I bought land near the fork of the river.
I had been compliant to the Indians being given a parcel
    of their own land.
Now I was spokesman for a missionary.
I believe.
I believe.
I WILL BELIEVE!

There was a prophecy in the open air—
On the cross I foresaw your praises and they appeared to me
    as promise.

Because you were with me in my suffering, you will be with me
when I reign.

Did that mean God gave Jesus a vision of the believers that would
believe on his name?
Is that why Brainerd endured discomfort and the danger
of his travels?

I, Tatamy, interpreter for David Brainerd, traveled with him
among my people.
I saw Brainerd's inclination to despondency and consumption.
I saw his excessive labors to speak to the Indians.
Often my dreams were troubled.

We had to let the Colonists take our land.
We had to know the message from God came through the people
who came to take our land.
It was more than some could endure.
They threw dust into the air before they walked away.

SIX

The First Epistle General of John

¹ That which was from the beginning, which we have heard, which we have seen with our eyes, which we have looked upon, and our hands have handled, of the Word of life; ² we have seen it, bear witness, ³ that which we have seen and heard declare unto you, fellowship with the Father and his Son Jesus Christ— [I was getting behind]— we have seen with our eyes handled the Word manifest as we bear witness with him bear that which we have seen declare his fellowship is with our fellowship—

I, Tatamy, had to say the text as I heard it from Brainerd.
I had to break the text as they broke the land.
To speak it.
Plow it.
Make it say what Brainerd said.
His words raised up as crop.
His crop raised up as words.

I spoke to the Natives.
I am divided as the river.
I myself am FORKED.
When one leg falls off the other will not stop growing.

SEVEN

Brainerd told the Indians about Hell.
Sometimes the words stopped in my mouth.
I had to think how to say them.
Brainerd looked at me— Say it just as I say it.
Speak my words in your language.
Do not change any of them.

You see them cry, I said.
You see them leave if they don't want to hear?
I AM telling them your words.
You ask me to change language.
You want your words to settle among ours, and change
    the structure.
You want our language to break apart.
You want to insert yours into it.
Why don't you hear what our language says?

I told Brainerd it was hard to say what he was preaching.
Hell was something we didn't know in our language.
Fire was ceremony— not torment.
To interpret was to make our language into something for which
    there were not words.
This message was beyond our language.

Where was the Lenape word for resurrection? I asked when we were on our horses riding to another encampment. How could I explain in a language which had no concept of it, and no word order for it?

EIGHT

Use of Ownership

[I]t is lawful now to take a land which none useth, and made use of it— Robert Cushman, Plymouth Colony, 1617

Go and walk through the land, and describe it, and come again to me. . .. And the men went and passed through the land, and described it. . . in a book. . . and came again to Joshua. . . and there Joshua divided the land— Joshua 18:8-10

Walk the land. Describe it. Own it with your words.
What is land? It is thought.
It is language that says, mine.
Land is a plow pulled by draft horses—
    the blade curved as a claw.
The crows overhead—
    their caws— the wooden cogs turning a ratchet wheel.
Land is a supply wagon.
An abundant row of crops.
Land is a pump handle.
A weapon.

A mold for lead balls.
Land is animal tracks along a dirt road.
Land is signature.
It is deed.   It is act.
Hear it talk to the river—
    the tree in the field
    a spike to hold down.

NINE

Why were the settlers divided between the Missionaries and the Colonists who knew how to use the language we didn't know against us? There were two sides to men. We had to swallow the differences. The injustice between them. The fork in the river.

Brainerd had reserve, yet could plunge into any group and speak his gospel. I was amazed that a weak, blundering man could bring a message that made Indians weep. He was wearing himself out— Preaching more than he had the strength to do. But that was the power of language. It came from his mouth. It went before him.

For years, I lived among the Colonists, moving from the place they called, New Jersey, to the Forks of the Delaware in Pennsylvania. Listening to them speak English. Learning it myself. Or what I could know of their words that were different to what I knew of my own words. I OWNED a tract of land. That was the leader of their words. OWN. Be in possession of. They worked their language like they worked their land. It was to publish crops. In Brainerd's case, it was words that reached the soul.

What was a soul? A Lenape woman proclaimed she did not know she had a soul. Brainerd said it was the breath of God that had been in us since the beginning when he took dust and breathed his breath into it. It was the shadow part of ourselves that woke when we accepted their God as our Savior. If it were true, why hadn't we known? Why hadn't our own guardian spirits told us? Why did we have to have these people tell us?

There were times when Brainerd preached, I could see the Darkness we were in, and beyond the Darkness, one Path to the Light World. It was the Path Brainerd told the Indians about. *Guttummaukalummeh wechaumeh kmeleh Ndah*— Have mercy on me, and help me to give you my heart. A wave continued to sweep over our meetings. Indians lay on the ground weeping. There was an awakening of something in them that Brainerd said belonged to God.

TEN

Didn't Brainerd know I should be on my farm working in the fields?— I, Tatamy

---

I woke in the night.
I heard someone knock.
I wasn't able to move for a moment.
Who was there?
Another knock.
I sat on the edge of the bed.
I went to the door of my cabin.
No one there but the bright moon.
The night drew me into it.
Was I still asleep?

I had told Brainerd I was a Christian.
He could not have an interpreter who did not understand
    his message.
It was hard enough to explain.
There was a God with the blessing of eternal life.
There was a God with eternal punishment.

He would kill and torture everyone who did not worship him.
A torture that extended from this life.
That began from it.

It's not that way, Brainerd argued.

But it's what you preach, I refuted.
Heaven or Hell.
Confess with your mouth[4] and you will see heaven.
Accept what the Colonists say— what we take with our words—
   it is ours.
That is the Indians' hell.
You preach a forked God, I told Brainerd.
A God divided as the river.
The Indians respond because they are desperate when caught
   in the fork of the Colonists' ways.

---

4. Romans 10:9

ELEVEN

I, Tatamy: a Walking Treaty

In 1687 William Penn proposed a "walking purchase" for Indian land. The Indians would sell their land as far as a man could walk in a day and a half. Or 30 miles. But Thomas and John Penn hired 3 men to walk in record time. Underbrush was cut from the path. The three men covered 60 miles in 36 hours.

I was sick.
I shivered.
I sweated.
I felt hot.
I was cold.
Nothing could warm me.
Nothing could cool.
My head swam.
I had nightmares of ghost-people gathered in the room.
Mesingw, one of the evil ones, was there.
I slept in the day.
I was awake at night.

I felt myself leave the earth.
I held to the covers so I would not go.

The dreams in my head were worse than wolves.
I thought I heard them eating bones.
But it was someone knocking.
Maybe it was no one again.
The knocking continued as it had the night before.

It was Brainerd who came to my cabin.
He needed me for another journey.
I was his interpreter.
It's still night, I said.
The stars were shining in the sky.
It's 4 am, he answered.

When he saw I was sick, he came into the cabin and prayed for me.
In my fever, I saw Brainerd cutting the brush for me.
I practiced running in my delirium.
The Nighthawk flew after me.
I kept running.
I covered twice what he thought I would.
Brainerd's voice troubled the waters and I stepped in.
Afterward, I believed more than I had before.
I was more confident of my salvation.
It was a profitable sickness.
If Brainerd would give up comfort to preach to a people that
    no one wanted, I could interpret for him.

I continued to be amazed at the reaction of those who heard his words.
Sometimes it was only one or two in an encampment.
Other times nearly the whole village accepted Brainerd's words, or seemed to.

As for the Colonists— they kept encroaching.
It was a word I learned from them.
As a wolf encroaches its prey.
As it crawls slowly up and leaps. To break the neck with its mouth. To devour.

TWELVE

Tatamy on the Brink of Despair

The lesser Size of Early ripe Corn yields an Ear not much larger than the Handle of a Case Knife... The larger Sort... as thick as a Child's Leg...[5]

Brainerd was dying, and yet he preached.
We traveled across creeks and gullies, pulling our horses up trails
    we couldn't ride.
We were in a thick forest.
We heard the *shurrrr* of leaves.
Birds were wild above us.
Sometimes, the trail disappeared, but I found it again.
We stepped across fallen trees.
We crossed marshes where beavers had blocked streams with
    their mounds.
We led the horses through the water.
I told Brainerd to stay on his horse to keep his boots and trousers
    dry, the hem of his coat.
But he would not.
Sometimes I had to help him on his horse.

    5. Beverly, Robert, *The History and Present State of Virginia*

I wondered if he wanted to die.
He seemed unafraid of the Indians.
Didn't he know we had attacked settlers and wiped out
    their pitiful settlements?

We passed a small clearing where a Lenape camp had been,
    but he didn't notice.
I think he already was blind to this world.

Several times, on a steep trail, we had to stop for him to rest.

I rode with Brainerd in the open rain.
At night, thunder tore the sky.
Streaks of lightning pierced.
We sat under the tarp.
I heard thunder answer thunder across the sky.
The way birds called and answered on a clear morning.
Often the horses startled.
We stood with them.
Brainerd's voice calmed me also.
I could believe in God because of the thunder.

In the morning, we rode again.
Brainerd stopped to cough as we traveled.
He stopped to cough during sermons.
He coughed again at night, yet preached the next day.
The Indians swallowed the light that shined in Brainerd's
    weak voice.
When Jesus saw him [cough] and knew [cough] he had been
    thus now a long time, he saith
Wilt thou [cough] be made whole?— John 5:6.
Beloved Christ, Author of our Faith. [cough]
    TRIUMPHANT over Sorrows.

Thirteen

We put bits in the horses' mouths and turn their whole body—
James 3:3

Wepu tb its i nth ehor se s'mou ths an dtu rn
the irw hol ebo dy—J ame s3:3

I used our stories to speak to my people.
Even the Sachem listened.
Because our stories were a semblance of what could not
    be spoken, but was nonetheless known.
There was a turtle that became the land.
A tree grew from its back.
We came from the roots of the tree.
The turtle was drawn with a coal from the fire to tell the story.
Whosoever drew the turtle was the one-who-told-the-story.
The past seemed to cover itself by what happened
    among opinions.
History lived in its versions.
Brainerd's history divided the land into furrows.
History was the crop that arises thereafter, always in
    the same straight rows.

I told the Lenape— God came from the tree also.

He was the tree.

He was the turtle.

There was rumbling from the Indians.

Brainerd looked at me.

He was suspicious of my translating.

The English language moved forward.

It had a goal it must reach.

The Indian language was the journey, often circling back before it went forward again.

He must have suspicioned that I wasn't translating exactly— but was translating in a way the Indians would understand.

Your stories are written in a book, I said.

A BOOK.

Always held in the same place and marked by numbers that WOULD NOT change.

Scripture is not open to change, Brainerd said.

A story lives by its changing, I answered.

This is not a story left to men, Brainerd insisted. It is from God.

I could get on my horse and LEAVE Brainerd with the people who could not understand his words.

I could leave him, and he would get lost in the woods.

Didn't he know to fear the wolf?

The bear?

The Indians who knew how to torture and kill?
Brainerd came to them with the message they should stop
 fighting and sit before the Lord.
Only it was me they listened to when he spoke.
I thought at times the warriors would kill me for the message
 I brought.
At one point, I knew several Indians followed us, but Brainerd
 seemed unaware of them.
Finally, I realized they were no longer there.
Maybe Brainerd's God had turned them back.

FOURTEEN

A number has no ears.

It has no story.

A number is service.

It is a mark bent or curved with other marks for purpose—

How many leagues across the water

How many ships

How many settlers in wagons

How many miles to the next village

How many and many until they fill the land.

Take ye the sum of the numbers and number them by numbers.

Numbers is a book called Numbers in THE BOOK.

So did everyone according to their numbers.

FIFTEEN

Tatamy in the Trough of Suffering

These fields are mine.
I could plow them with the twig of my arm.

GUTTUMMAUKALUMMEH
WECHAUMEH KMELEH NDAII!!

I wait to be changed into your image, LORD,
    at the resurrection of those who believe.

I, Tatamy, a statesman to the Colonists,
    a traitor to my people.

SIXTEEN

Those nights alone in my car unlatching the shore.

The Spirit of Tatamy Speaks after the Death of Tatamy

My cabin now
    belongs to someone else.
They have two children and a three-
    legged dog
    and will take down
    the dead tree and
    repair
    the roof.

So much I loved it
    I let it go.

THE CONVERSION OF HE GOES FIRST, DAVID PENDLETON OAKERHATER, CHEYENNE[6]

---

6. First Native American Anglican to be included in the book of *Lesser Feasts and Facts of the Episcopal Church.*

Fort Marion Prison, St. Augustine, Florida, 1875-78[7]

Notes to the Living Father, you brought us this.
You showed them the water to cross.
They kept coming. We resisted.
We should fold up our teepees? Leave the Great Plains?
They pushed until we had nowhere to go.

Holy Lord, the buffalo roam now in the other world.
You have them with you there.
You gather the dead from the earth.
You have it your way.

We rode to Fort Sill with a white flag.
We came to captivity by your hand.

The flag flopped before our eyes.
We eat the surrender you give us.

We wore leg irons. We rode the train. The boat.
After a long journey we walked into Fort Marion on the ocean.
They cut our hair.
Covered our legs with trousers.
Our chests with blue coats. We were made to look like them.
Fervent Lord hear our prayer. We are not them.

    7. An abandoned fort where 72 warriors were taken at the end of the Plains Indian Wars and attempts were made to educate and evangelize.

If I had a horse I would ride into the sea.

Notes to the horse— keep moving your legs.
Surely the boats are horses to these men.

We stand in our soldier suits.
We march around the courtyard of the fort in their
 military maneuvers.
Our fathers would not know us.

There were stories of the land
 stopping at the water that walked where it went.

I had seen the water. I felt it moving in my dreams.
We have an ocean within us.

**Notes to Mrs. Mather at the fort
to teach us English.**

Your words pull threads from the water.
Your words make leg irons for our words to wear.

Your words are a thicket. A little copse of trees.

SNAKE BITE ME. [actual words He Goes First wrote]

A buffalo calf stepped on a snake. I felt the bite of it.
The next world near.

Mrs. Mathers asked what I was writing.
I said the bite of the snake in my leg though it bit the buffalo calf.
There was sameness of land— of sky— of buffalo.
I was trying to find the sameness of writing.

If I was on the Plains I would not write.
I would hide in the thicket. I would become buffalo.
My hide left for the hide hunters to take.
That is not correct, she said shesaidshesaid.

Notes to Mrs. Mather—
I hide in the thicket I make with your language.
Therein a snake that would bite—
    that would transform the buffalo calf into a being
The Maker would lift in his hands to his New World.
The calf with the Plains for a back— the thicket for a tail—
    an ocean for its head.

After the Red River Indian Wars of the 1870's—

We sit in your prison at Fort Marion, Lord.
We have come for lessons we already know.

They will not hear us, but we are to hear them.
It is their world now.

Bishop Whipple stands before us speaking—
    not knowing where we came from.

If he had seen a scalped head.
If he had seen the skinned buffalo.
If he had seen the piles of hides.
If he had heard our cries—

Sometimes I see Whipple as a Holy Man
    when he turns white as a blizzard.
His words are buffalo on the Plains.
They are a blur of whirlwind.

He is fighting for your kingdom, Lord.
His words are a thin trail of water in the Red River in dry weather.

Sometimes I see Bishop Whipple in a breech-clot.
His face painted red and black with a stripe across his forehead.

I am lost in the wind, Lord. I am come apart.
Take my life.
The ocean is another sky.

The Easement of Dream

One night I flew above the clouds.
I thought at first I was over the water.
I often watched the waves roll into shore after their long journey.
But it was the clouds that were rippled and not the water.

The dream moved away from the clouds until I saw them from
    a distance.
The clouds were ragged on top as a line of trees.

I had flown back all night over the Red River.

There was another world.
I had known it on the Plains.

We sat at a table at the fort.
We learned some English. Writing and speaking.
We war danced for tourists.
We made souvenirs. We sold our ledger book drawings.

Still it was not another day. Still. Still.

Notes to the still—
The drawings we made. Of fort. Of horse.
Of boat in the bay.
Of vacant sea. Was blowing. Would not stop.

Notes to the buffalo—
There was nothing we could do.
I tell you we could not stop the soldiers and hide hunters
    from killing.

Notice. Notice. To the soldiers.
There is above you a line of tress waiting.

After Fort Marion

I studied English. I studied scripture.[8]

The enemy came at night to question. To ridicule.

I was a Bow String Warrior. Now I wore a suit minus breech-clot minus long hair minus buffalo minus teepee minus Sun Dance minus the wolf howling minus prairie grass minus whirlwind minus bow and arrow minus wives and children minus the horse that was the same as myself. Minus. Minus. Minusminusminusminusminus. The battle now was in the small bladder bag of the head above the feet the arms the neck coiled with snakes if you'd seen a head struck open in battle.

I heard the Old World speak. I would return to the Plains minus the Medicine Shield. I had to give up the Old World push aside the fear of the new. It was the same as my first war against the Otoes and Missouries on the Little Blue River.

---

8. Mary Douglass Burnham, an Episcopal deaconess, arranged for He Goes First to continue his education at St. Paul's Church in Paris Hill, New York where Reverend J.B. Wicks baptized and confirmed him as David Pendleton Oakerhater. Oakerhater was baptized again at Grace Episcopal Church in Syracuse and ordained as a deacon in 1881. He chose his name after the Biblical David, and Pendleton after the family that provided funding for his education. It is still not clear whether He Goes First was falsely accused of crimes in the last skirmish in the Red River Wars that sent him to Fort Marion.

Notes to Darlington Agency Indian Territory.

I stood before my people with an Episcopal Book
    of Common Prayer.
I had been a war leader.
Now I was an Episcopal Deacon.

I told them of a new road. They could know the journey.

The people winced. They looked away.

The Prayer Book was my Dream Shield
    my Red Shield Bowstring Headdress I wore now
    with a Standing Feather and Yellow Porcupine Quills
    with Black Ends.

I had been broken yet I stood as if I was not.

The soldiers came as prairie fire. They left a blackened field.

The ones who followed taught us the world had more than
    one road.
They taught the Maker had more than one name.[9]

    9. Oakerhater's names— Noksowist— Bear Going Straight— He Goes Straight— He Goes First— Sun Dancer— Making Medicine— Oakahaton— O-kuh-ha-tuh— David Pendleton Oakerhater. Born c. 1848 Indian Territory— died August 31, 1931, Watonga, Oklahoma

How Could I Say What Has No Word for It

The Medicine Lodge Treaty and other negotiations
    had not worked
    and would not work because they were not meant to work.
There would be no shared land.
They sat down to tea to discuss ideas to ratify more treaties
    and more treatiestreatiestreaties
    until they were running from our ears.
So many gophers from their holes.
The quarter moon a stirrup to ride the Plains.
I could fly in the blowing air. That summer a plane with
    two wings buzzed the field—
    the pasture actually— a man stood on the wings as
    a winged being of old visions.
It was a memory of crossed lodge-poles that left only memory.
I was at Whirlwind Mission Indian School in Indian Territory.
The field matron reported trachoma in the students.
The Indians let the land allotments fall through their hands.
There were government regulations against Indians camping
    on mission-ground.
The baptisms yes— but confirmations lacking.
We knew the outcome of our wars was too much to bear
    at one time.
We had fought, but defeat was this kingdom— this glory
    in the world to come.

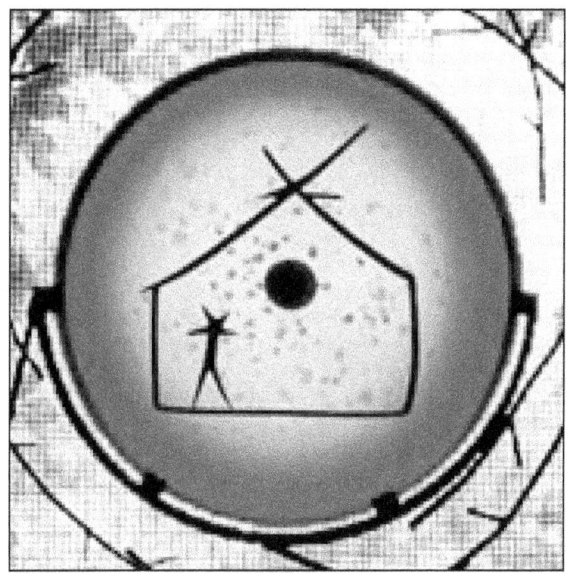

Oakerhater Window, St. Paul's Cathedral, Oklahoma City, by Tlingit glass artist, Preston Singletary

Acknowledgments, Notes and Bibliography

THE FLYING HEAD and NEW ENGLAND INDIANS

Gratefulness to The American Antiquarian Society, Worcester, Massachusetts, for the July 2020 John and Charlotte Brown Creative Artist Fellowship for the writing of the first two sections.
July 3, 2020

It was at AAS that I saw "The Flying Head," and interpreted it as the way Christianity first looked to the Native American. Reprint in public domain.

The Worcester Review, Volume 43, Artists in the Archives, Part 2, 2022, for "1. Cockenoe [Montauk]," "2. Wowaus or James Printer [Nipmuc]," "3. John Sassamon [Massachusett]," and "4. Job Nesuton [Massachusett]"

Research in a time of Covid—
Landings are never easy. The Pilgrims knew.

July 3, 2020
I left Kansas around 9:00 on a Friday morning. I drove across Missouri, Illinois, Indiana, past Columbus, Ohio, where I slept in a rest area just west of Zanesville. I had driven 691 miles. Maybe it

is the virus epidemic. The place was nearly filled with trucks and cars for the night, not wanting to stay in motels, I suppose. The next morning, I continued on I-70 east to 79 north, to I-80 east across the hills of Pennsylvania, to 81 north in eastern Pennsylvania, to 84 east into New York, Connecticut, and Massachusetts. As I neared Boston, I cut north on I-90 to 290 to Worcester. I thought Salisbury Street was a junction to the highway, but it was not. I passed Worcester and stopped to put 4 Regent Street into the GPS. The sun was bright in my eyes. I followed traffic moving swiftly along a curving street. Then came Salisbury, and then Regent Street and The American Antiquarian Society. I had driven 743 miles the second day.

Burned out, unsure of what was ahead. At last I had arrived. If in parts that also would have to be unpacked. A journey across America's blessed Interstates in my Ford.

Gratefulness to Kim Toney and her online exhibition of the Algonquian Bible. https://amerianantiquarian.org/EnglishtoAlgonquian

Thank you—Nan Wolverton, Dan Boudreau, Brianne Barrett, and Laura Elizabeth Pope who set the 1663 Indian Bible on my table like a substantial loaf of bread. Thank you to James Moran and his explanation of the printing press at AAS, which is part of the Wowaus or James Printer section.

At the American Antiquarian Society, I wrote a hybrid work. Broken into fragments. A semblance. A trace. A reductionism. The pieces taken down, almost disassembled.

I have a writing desk in my house that was a barn door. Where there were small holes, the craftsman used brown filler. Then sanded and oiled the door. When I sit at my desk in the light, I can see the filler. It is the work I do for history with its missing parts.

Language takes us through its filter of woods from one place to another transformed by weather whether snow, rain, drought, heat, cold, the abundance of leaves in summer, the lack of them in winter, and all the subsequent upheavals thereto.

It is memory that takes the form of weather.

Bibliography

Indian Bible, 1661-1663, Translated into Algonquian, John Eliot, printed by the Commissioners of the United Colonies in New England, Samuel Green and Marmaduke Johnson, Cambridge, MDCLXIII

The Indian Grammar Begun, or, an Essay to bring the Indian Language into RULES, for the Help of such as desire to Learn the same, for the furtherance of the Gospel among them, by John Eliot, Cambridge, Printed by Marmaduke Johnson, 1666

Holy Bible, Old and New Testaments, Together with the Apocrypha, Translated out of the Original Tongues, McCarty & Davis, Philadelphia, 1881

A Grammar of the Massachusetts Indian Language, John Eliot, First printed by Marmaduke Johnson, Cambridge, 1666. Later printed with Introductory Notes by John Pickering, Phelps and Farnham, Boston, 1822

Bibliography of the Algonquian Languages, James Constantine Pilling, Washington Government Printing Office, 1891

Some Helps for the Indians Showing Them How to Improve their natural Reason, To know the True God, and the true Christian Religion,

1. By leading them to see the Divine Authority of the Scriptures
2. By the Scriptures the Divine Truth necessary to Eternal Salvation

Undertaken At the Motion, and published by the Order of the Commissioners of the United Colonies, by Abraham Pierson, Examined and approved by Thomas Stanton Interpreter-Generall to the United Colonies for the Indian Language, and by some others of the most able Interpreters amongst us. London, Printed by N. Simmons, 1659

The Light appearing more and more towards the perfect Day. Or, a farther Discovery of the present state of the Indian in New-England, Concerning the Progresse of the Gospel amongst them. Manifested by Letters from such as preacht to them there. Published by Henry Whitfield, late Pastor to the Church of Christ at Gilford in New-England, who came late thence, LONDON, Printed by T.R. & E.M. for John Bartlet, and are to be sold at the Gilt Cup, near St. Austins gate in Pauls Churchyard, 1651

The glorious progress of the Gospel, amongst the Indians of New England: Manifested by three letters, under the hand of that famous instrument of the Lord Mr. John Eliot, and another from Mr. Tomas Mayhew. London, Printed for Hannah Allen in Popes-Head-Alley 1649, In a volume of Indian Tracts or Indian History, having paper made from old linen clothing laid on wires, pressed, rubbed, but the lines still visible.

The Indian Primer or The First Book By which Children may know truly to read the Indian Language. Printed by B. Green, 1720

Indiane Primer Afuh NEGONNEYEUUK, Ne nashpeMukkiesog Woh tauogwunnamuhkuttee ogketamunnate Indiane Unnontoowaonk. Printeuun nasope B. Green, 1720

"The Path of the King James Version of the Bible in Iroquoia," Scott Manning Stevens, *Prose Studies Journal*, April 1, 2012—

John Eliot was well practiced in translation between numerous European languages. But Eliot's task [in 1666] was an even greater challenge because he would first have to invent an orthographic system and discern the inherent grammar of a language that hitherto had never been written in alphabetic form. . . It is not a simple case of finding the verb and its subject, but rather a case of reinventing one's concept of how language functions. . .Even the notion of how written words were to be divided in a language that combined nouns and verbs as seemingly single utterances had not been completely resolved.

[By permission of Scott Manning Stevens from the *Path of the King James Version of the Bible in Iroquoia*.]

Removable Type, Histories of the Book in Indian Country, 1663-1880, Phillip H. Round, The University of North Carolina Press, 2010

The Common Pot, Lisa Brooke, Indigenous Americas Series, University of Minnesota Press, 2008

Our Beloved Kin, Lisa Brooks, Yale University Press, 2018

Memory Lands, King Philip's War and the Place of Violence in the Northeast, Christine M. Delucia, Yale University Press, 2018

I, TATAMY

To an Unnamed Foundation for the Arts

Recently, I read *The Life and Diary of David Brainerd*, 1718-1747, a missionary to the New England Indians, edited by Jonathan Edwards. What I missed in the book were the voices of the Indians. I wanted to read their responses to Brainerd's ministry. Their version. Their perspective. Of course, not many Native voices were recorded. I decided to concentrate on Moses Tenda Tauta-my, the Lenape interpreter for David Brainerd.

I am applying for a grant to travel to eastern Pennsylvania around the Forks of the Delaware, where Brainerd and Tatamy traveled. I NEED to be on the land to pick up his voice. I'm interested in the overlay of history. I write from the intersection of that which was going, and that which is here. The retrieval of historical voices that did not have a chance to speak has been my work for YEARS.

I travel to places no one sees. I drive from dawn to dark until a nubbin appears, which is a dirt-clod from which the first words fall, which is the earth on which my small plot forms. All I own is back where I left. All that is ahead is the voice I seek.

I want to explore the narrative of Tatamy. The interior landscape. The stone of experience. A man of reconciliation who would consider the turbulence of ideas. This is WHAT I WANT. Tatamy traveled with David Brainerd. He heard his words. He interpreted to the Lenape.

I am interested in first-person narratives of what could have been thought or said. To do this, I HAVE to travel to places they traveled. It is the land that carries the words of their memory. My work is not a ghosting that brings back a semblance of the historical voices that could have been somewhere in the neighborhood of what-their-voices-could-have-been.

I go one place to get to another. My research is inadvertent. It is an indirect method. I write another history to write my own.

Tatamy moved from Mercer County, northern New Jersey, to the Forks of the Delaware in Pennsylvania, as the land between the Lehigh River and the Delaware was called, where he farmed 315-acres of tract land. I want to stop in the area around Easton, Allentown and Susquehanna in Pennsylvania. I know the land has changed, as it always has on my historical travels, but enough of the past endures that I get the ideas I need. I AM ASKING FOR TRAVEL FUNDS TO LOOK AT THE LAND. I want to go to the place the Lenape called, *Lechewuekink*, where-the-water-divides, as the world was dividing for Tatamy and the Native people, as it still seems to be dividing.

The grant was denied. The deed was dead. I got in my car, slept in rest areas at night. Found Tatamy standing on his land.

Some of the pieces were published in a 4 x 9½ broadside, *Oscimal at First Light*, Azusa Pacific University, 2013. Acknowledgment to William Catling for *Turning from that which will not heal* for the cover of the broadside. Reprint permission by the sculptor. William Catling, williamcatling.com

The Journal of Poetry and Poetics, Vol 1, No 4, 2013, for "Use of Ownership"

Traces: Sand and Snow in Symbiosis, 2024, for "Use of Ownership" and "A Number Has No Ears"

Bibliography

The Life and Diary of David Brainerd, 1718-1747, a missionary to the New England Indians, edited by Jonathan Edwards, Hendrickson Publishers, 2006

Tatamy Afterword

Tawpoot

And I saw a new heaven and earth,
for the first heaven and earth were passed away,
and there was no more sea— Revelation 21:1

Lord, I see you in a wet suit. A name tattooed on your thigh. I don't know how far I can go in admiring you, in uncovering your blessed self. I don't know how persistently I can present my case. Drive me in a roadster with a wolf hound in the backseat to the cliff above the water leaping from the shore rocks. I see a cabana on the shore for changing, though I hear there is no ocean there. Where will the fish go? What are whale songs if not praises to your majesty? Let me argue for the sprawl of ocean. It was the misfit earth that chin-strapped you to a tree. It was the sea you walked across. I don't want pleasantries as much as life instructional as a flannel-graph in a church basement. I'm stoked on the theater of the surf. Your tender jellyfish and hard-core judgments. Your heavy metal door no one can open but you. Maybe fight will be removed when we enter de-finned into your heaven and the beloved sea memorialized before your throne as Waterford crystal.

TriQuarterly Literary Journal for "Tawpoot"
under the title, "Blessed Apparel"

THE CONVERSION OF HE GOES FIRST

Acknowledgment to *The Missouri Review*, Jeffrey E. Smith Editor's Prize, 2019, Finalist for "The Conversion of He Goes First." The eight-part sequence poem was published online as *The Missouri Review* Poem of the Week, June 17, 2019

"The Conversion of He Goes First" was read at an offsite reading hosted by *The Missouri Review* at the Associated Writing Programs Conference in San Antonio, Texas, March 5, 2020, the last conference before the Covid-19 virus shut-down subsequent AWP conferences for two years.

Reprint permission for the Oakerhater Window, St. Paul's Cathedral, Oklahoma City, by Preston Singletary.

Bibliography

Fort Marion Prisoners and the Trauma of Native Education, Diane Glancy, University of Nebraska Press, 2014

Back Cover

Acknowledgment for the poem, "4 x 4," to *Traces: Sand & Snow in Symbiosis*, Anthology of African, North American / European Poets, edited by Jeffrey Alan Lockwood and Mohamed Abdellahi Ould BABAH E. Horma O. Abd Eljelil, Middle Creek Press, 2024.

www.ingramcontent.com/pod-product-compliance
Lightning Source LLC
Chambersburg PA
CBHW071732040426
42446CB00011B/2334